DREAMS OF DIASPORA

poems by

S.K. Rancy

Finishing Line Press
Georgetown, Kentucky

DREAMS OF DIASPORA

Copyright © 2023 by S.K. Rancy
ISBN 979-8-88838-160-1 First Edition
All rights reserved under International and Pan-American Copyright Conventions. No part of this book may be reproduced in any manner whatsoever without written permission from the publisher, except in the case of brief quotations embodied in critical articles and reviews.

Publisher: Leah Huete de Maines
Editor: Christen Kincaid
Cover Art: Edouard Duval Carrié, Artist / Curator, "Tropical Convention with Head 2"
Author Photo: Jemille T Rancy
Cover Design: Elizabeth Maines McCleavy

Order online: www.finishinglinepress.com
also available on amazon.com

Author inquiries and mail orders:
Finishing Line Press
P. O. Box 1626
Georgetown, Kentucky 40324
U. S. A.

Table of Contents

La Florida 1

Flight 3

Re-Signification of Gold Grillz as War Helms 5

Slaves Talk of America 7

Decolonization in the Context of Economic Dependence . 10

Dream Sequence with Fanon 14

After Basquiat 16

In the light between being and becoming 19

Diasporic Fever Dream 22

Portrait of the Sea as 25

Decolonial Poetry Is 28

Banana Country: A Litany 29

Eucharist 32

Portrait of Love as Revolution 34

Love Song for a Country 37

Ulysses Seeks Ithaca in the Antilles 39

Homecoming 44

Kreyòl 47

Veneration 51

Flatbush and 7th Ave, 2021 54

Hymn to Haiti 55

Acknowledgements 59

fanmi mwen: tout sa pou ou

How often have I lain beneath rain on a strange roof, thinking of home.
—William Faulkner, *As I Lay Dying*

I do not live inside you, I bear
my house inside me, everywhere
—Derek Walcott, *Omeros*

La Florida

        I.

Land of flowers
land
of police shootings
& black-baby murders ,
where tongues unfold
over campfire
a history of horrors ,
of slave-back scarred thick
like leather , under iron & whip
lynchings & beatings ,
pallid Seminoles
fleeing
under terror of pitchfork & gunfire
into swampland
900 miles of
death
a trail of tears
&
American eagles
atop red pickup trucks , flapping
boisterous star-spangled flags , rippling :
this is America , land of the free
gee-golly-tarnation God made this country
for me

        II.

No —
for *us*

Listen : cicadas
singing

        III.

Land

of immigrants
Port
of Spain , port of riches ,
port of princes ,
peninsula
of fantastical
fauna y flora , bursting at the seams
Everglade swamp-fire & flamingos , apt
strange starfish & crabs
luminescent
scuttling over moonlit sands ,
towering pines
bristling in sea-breeze
alien dolphins leaping
in the night
great glistening leviathans(
There is something underneath the surface —)
mango and okra
roti and curry
reggaetón and hip-hop
pikliz and sazón
poetry & palm trees
rum and rum
jump-rope and slang-speak
black-neck-cookin' heat
can't catch the beat
can't catch these hands
can't catch these rhymes
rind
of orange , lime
smelling of ocean
sound of seashell
a conch echoing a song
of homeland
across the sea
where are we?
what is identity? an immigrant
black boy begs
adrift in the waves
churn
sink
drown

Flight

> *Far from fading away, it appears that prisons are here to stay.*
> —introduction to Michelle Alexander's *The New Jim Crow*

I remember
the way asphalt cracked & spit
in summer heat
underfoot a heavenly host
my cousins and me
bright black seraphim with
brush cuts and hair twists clasped in clips
tight, the way children should be held
donned and decked
in K-Swiss sneakers and baggy 2004 t-shirts
branded Ecko Unlimited, echoes unlimited
our voices were loud, and first-generation
American
& we chased each other
from street to street
roamed through fields of grass
till evening
wandered aimlessly without fear
of losing ourselves, only each other
danced beneath Florida stars
on the basketball court, like Michael or Wade
limbs birdlike
& twice as swift
ate pickled hot sausages made
in the back of somebody's momma's borrowed van
probably
& it burned good
the roofs of our mouths swelling
like lungs
before the shout

For years
I couldn't quite figure out
why the park basketball hoops

were one day conspicuously gone
but learned soon
what it meant to be
a black American
see now
what we must have been
to them
neighborhood gang
menacing
unruly
unwanted
colossi — they feared our greatness
even then
even when
we were wide-eyed & wondrous
& wondering incredulous
at the white cop who leapt from his car
hand on his gun
& saw us
standing on the concrete seeing him
small fingers gripping the Spalding
& then all those black boys
like angels
flew

Re-Signification of Gold Grillz as War Helms

from the bedside table
don
the gilded,golden
armor : ward against
disrespect

    "you ain't got no shine
    Frank Ocean-listenin ass
    you soft"

subversion's too difficult a task &
every temple has a façade

facial decorative ,
    mask adorning
the fangs
    brag the ornament,
menace the mouth : let them see
    you have teeth

// break

bone
before they mistake you
for brittle (unresistant
victim)

    break even
    your own fingers
    re-forge the mold
    clamber anew
    from
    that hulking corpse

this is your
    reality
subjectivity(damned social theorists)

        Truth

come , let them see it —
       that you   command
death

                                      off-stage : gangsta , inconsolably
                                      weeping

Slaves Talk of America

> *Freeing yourself was one thing,*
> *claiming ownership*
> *of that freed self was*
> *another.*
> —Toni Morrison, *Beloved*

I was born in a city
they named

                    Plantation —
                    pry open the wound

        in the memory of lineage
        my ancestors

    confused & restless like flies
    stare up

through darkness
from the bowels of ships

                    white-eyed, tongueless
                    a premonition

        in the islands
        they tied our limbs

to horses & tore
our bones & ligaments

                    from meat
                    in the Congo

        they chopped off our fingers
        & in Virginia

    they still pretend we danced
    on the auction blocks

    crying out hallelujah
    salvation at last

                         is this what your god
                          calls paradise?

            breeding us
            chattel like cattle

                    in a hot cesspit
                    dumb mute animals

    from farm to table
    to be devoured

                    sucking up our marrow
                    cracked chicken bones

    scattered
    to the nameless wind

                    flowering the dirt
                    with carrion

            the soil in Florida
            still thick & wet

                    with our blood
                    the trees

    still bloated with bodies
    hidden in the leaves

                          and you think
                          we would forget that?

            and you think
            we should forget that?

        maroons in the Caribbean
        cooked their colonizers

    at the spit
    yet every day in America

I am a hunted slave
runaway in a hoodie

      running through
      the whipping reeds

   a chorus of insects
   moaning

      either their fury or praise
      who can say

the night full of noises
& the air listening

    every night I hear it —
    feet, running

      a thundering
      in my flesh

    like all the slaves
    in my blood

banging on my teeth
still begging

        to be free

Decolonization in the Context of Economic Dependence

Distraught, Hilarion observed this phantasmagoric scene
—Jacques Stéphen *Alexis, General Sun, My Brother* (tr. Carrol F. Coates)

Build them
a cage
beat them,until
even the blood runs
black, cadaveric, necrotic

BARK "work, dog,
on pain of death"

Hug the fruits of labor —
coffee, banana, cocoa, tobacco, cassava —
to your pockets
& erect empires
Babel-rivaling hubris

When the subhuman
savages
dance(scattering
pig's blood into the flame
inciting frenzy)when
the masses
politicize//edify//mobilize
awake —

    ungrateful bastards
    is this not
    Utopia ?

shoot them .

decimate their
'culture'

denigrate
their claim to humanism
bury their bodies
in the deepest,darkest crypts of
non-History
à la Trouillot

then
dismantle the metropolis
that jewel
of empire ;
withdraw,cowed
to cries of

"¡libertad!"
"freedom!"
"egalité!"
"Trotsky!"
"People's Republic!"
"socialism!"

from the nascent nation a state
                        of anxiety
arises: a trembling infant's
fist
& the infant must
eat .

watch them
take up your abandoned factories
modes of production
trade markets and routes
yes eat yes generate
they will find a circumspect
business partner
in you (what
weakened state
would willingly deny
a customer

?)

morality and intellectualism are a dream
the ideals of fraternity
crumble & fall away
under the weight
of need

yes yes you will build
your utopian people's state
surely(eventually
)but now
eat : gnash your teeth
participate in the global economy
these engines of power
are already here
& you must produce
& sell
to grow

capitalism
is in your blood
the legacy of (y)our history
no one escapes
the vestiges of colonialism
the brand on the body:on the mind
wisps of
smoke,lingering

they have dismantled
the cage

        //crescendo of applause//

only to stand
in the glittering fenced field
beneath
a dream of sunlight
cast on a cave wall (

the image is not the object

)

the colonized subject
is a curious,fascinating
creature
let us study him
as
he works

Dream Sequence with Fanon

Scene : two men in suits seated in a café

FANON : Listen — the social revolution cannot draw its poetry
from the past

                                              POET : Meaning?

FANON : Marx ! Disalienation is only possible for the few, reject —
this reality is not
definitive

                POET : Ivory towers replete with comfortable seats ; where
                is the work?

FANON : I am talking of untethering

                POET : I am always breaking at the seams

FANON : Colonial past is part but
does not define
us

                POET : melancholy rivers bear us on
                Inevitability

FANON : Walcott , Roumain?

                POET : Machiavelli , Woolf

FANON : Past is structure ,
        trajectory , form — but destiny?

                POET : I am in the world

FANON : Yes

                POET : Endlessly creating
                        myself

FANON : Metaphysics of the self , not
the material

        POET : Jazz is an aether into which
        I dissolve

FANON : Yes

        POET : The burden of form falls away

FANON : Yes

        POET (standing) : I am a hurricane soaked in leaves
        and dews

FANON (clutching his temples , weeping) : Yes , yes

        POET : Act now , act now ,
        act now

After Basquiat

I.   *Obnoxious Liberals (1982)*

Beautiful black child

    head adorned

with a halo of stars :

I see you

    I understand

Yes

    I am screaming too

They sold you —

    You ,

who strived

    to break

their glass castle

    & show

those obnoxious liberals

    their own pretentious , perverse , grotesque

absurdity ;

    You ,

who screamed

        that Man

Love

        the Soul

Blackness itself

        is not

a commodity

        to be sold

NOT FOR SALE
NOT FOR SALE
NOT FOR SALE

        But

the name of the game is

        Late Capitalism

& everything

        is a product , anything

can make a buck

        for them

II.   *Untitled (1982)*

$110.5 million at auction at Sotheby's

        for the radiant child , a vial of his blood

bottled for splendor —

   a titan

achievement , a monstrous

   warping .

But they can't take , can't sell

   this :

rustle of brush on canvas ,

   an echo

of Ravel's Bolero

   or Miles's Bitches Brew ;

memories over beers with lovers and friends ,

   all bruised lips and free foreheads ;

and the spirit of the world

   of ancestors

of inspiration

   & History

moving through you , which

   in the end

is truly
   Yourself .

In the light between being and becoming

       i.

Walk beneath a rind
          of moon
remnants of a god's eye
          roving wild,
imposing constructions
          oscillating ideologies//

Tell me :

    Where is the Real?

    ii.

In that light
Black skin gleams

Starlit warrior
the hand holding
the pistol in your mouth
is yours

but it need not
be —
tragicomedy (there is no humor
in it) : your story need not be
this

Bullets
do not
peel off the skin (though
they will try
)
they glance off —
sound : rain pinging
on a tin roof

by the sea
This body of music
is home

Surge
Throw down your enemy
You are not
the enemy
You are human

In moonlight
you are silver
a fish   darting
There is no shimmering skin
so precious   as yours

America
has made another business
of selling you
your labor
your prison cell

Who are you?
Whose are you?
Whose chains
do you bear?

       iii.

Delimit identity

       Decolonize consciousness

What is fluid

       is never rigid

save the body's humors

   in death (

this

   is not your death)

Starlit warrior

   The back

bunches, ripples

   shackles break

and fall away

   The ancients smile down

& all the spirits laugh

   Your voice is

a fist

   smashing the moon's face

Diasporic Fever Dream

> *I speak the rage of overflowing waters*
> —Franketienne, *Ready to Burst* (tr. Kaiama L. Glover)

The river
splinters
its many
tributaries,
veins feeding
new shores

The cutting stone
juts
in the riverbed :
the crux
of colonialism
is dispersion

        torrential   forces

                  expelling

     p a r t i c u l a t e matter

each sphere

is a world

a sphere of identity

    aside: how many spheres
    do the post-colonized juggle?

in America you are
Black
blickity blickity Black
but home you are Caribbean
not like

those Americans
those *vakabon*
thugs
scum

      because Western racism
      sews itself into even
      the black psyche (
         see Fanon//fruitful discourse)

your tongue
is too heavy
too American
for your own language
but// you are not
the hyphenated-American
America
demands you be

enough hearing
the Artibonite River
thundering in your dreams
hearing in your mouth
Taíno screams
echoing

to s t r i n g yourself
across culture
is to split the flesh,
wound the sacred psyche
on barbed
existential dread

      how many spheres
      can you occupy(
      like they occupied
      us?)

let us count
the masks

or else
be all of your faces
not one — and be done
set aside
the analytical frameworks
the race/class theory
the history
of gunpowder sugar rain

semiotics
dictates:
symbols have only
the meanings we give them

& History
is a symbol
of power

Let your history
be
what you shape it :
let it be that : let it be
yours

Portrait of the Sea as

> For there was the sea, and on the other side of the sea
> was the world
> —Gabriel García Márquez, *The General in His Labyrinth* (tr. Edith Grossman)

    I.

Memory:

        The great powerful titan

lumbering through

        the dark

uncertain of its steps

        knowing only its own

inconstant

        beautiful

wavering

    II.

The Haitian rebels do not waver
on the plains, nor
on the mountaintop, overlooking
the waves
not even at the galleon approaching
as General Leclerc or Francisco Arango(

        it is all
        the same, history's oppressors
        coalesce

)look on from the bow
the eye steady, steely, oppressive —
blue as

The sea

crashes
thunders, thrashes
in its cradle
where legends will be born
of blood and fury
and sabers will quiver
in pursuit of liberty
or death

The salt-spray
stings
The flesh weeps,
an open wound
in the collective unconscious
surging, crying
their names:
Toussaint Louverture
Jean-Jacques Dessalines
Alexandre Pétion
Henri Christophe
remembering always
these four
gilded kings

In the sea
lies
the identity of the colonized
the buried bones
of history
whispering their song
& waiting
to be heard

III.

The sea

is eternal
prevails over men
subsumes all history
in sand and surf
To gaze into the sea
is to reconcile the totality
& insignificance
of man

generation & destruction :
forever ending & unending

Collapse

                breathe

break

                live !

The sea
is our history
The sea
is the sea

Decolonial Poetry Is

Decolonial poetry is
decolonial
Poetry is decolonial
Poetry is   Is decolonial poetry
decolonial
Is poetry decolonial
Is decolonial decolonial Is
decolonial poetry Is
poetry poetry Is is
is
Is
not
performative
Is not jargon
Is not theory
or ideology
Is praxis

                                      There is a time for text & a time
                                                    for the act
                                                    Iamb I am
                                                      The time
                                                        is now
                                                        & now
                                                        & now

Banana Country: A Litany

> Here I am
> poet
> adolescent
> in pursuit of an immense dream of love and liberty
> —René Depestre, "Me Voici" (tr. from the French)

    i.

Haitians still whisper the Dictator's name. A phantom in the fields. Malevolent echo in the mountains. A werewolf snatching up infants from their cribs. A name become myth. Transmogrification is a type of magic.

And what of disappearing?

    ii.

Marxist-poets once marched the streets. Romantic student-philosophers corralling the peasantry to unite like the fingers of a fist. Drawing the Dictator's ire.

There are no Marxist-poets now. Flesh feeding worm and loam.

    iii.

Di·as·po·ra. *Noun.* The dispersion of a people.

Look how Aeneas flees a burning Ilium.

    iv.

In Chile, the ex-pat poet befriends Pablo Neruda. Over coffee they discuss poetry and war. He imagines they are their forefathers, Alexandre Pétion and Simón Bolívar, plotting liberation. Time is a repetitive fiction: circuitous, elliptical orbit.

In the mountains of Cuba, he fights alongside Che Guevara and writes poetry under starlight and gunfire. At night, sitting atop the seawall in Havana and staring out into a hungry abyss, he dreams of a free Caribbean.

On a grassy hill beside the sea, Derek Walcott is still dreaming. He will never awaken.

v.

Then, the trembling.

vi.

Broken earth. A shuddering of mountains. Landscape of death.

Wreckage of a shattered presidential palace thrust up into dust-filtered sunlight, white & gleaming bone. Cholera in the river, the blood. Children run barefoot through the streets. The bells of what cathedrals remain issue their lament.

vii.

After the rupture: an absurdist farce of democracy. US diplomats intervene. A singer dancing in his briefs becomes puppet president. A cadre of bald vampires in suits suckles blood from a hot womb of earth.

The children across the sea do not return.

viii.

The children across the sea long to return. Their parents, haunted by memory in exile, forbid it.

ix.

Dream of an island. Under a glare of sun, air rippling like molten glass. Sweet pungent perfume of mango and guava assaulting the senses. Everywhere hyacinths, acacias, bougainvillea. Furious flamboyant, bursting into riot. Iguanas and lizards utter their dry croaks. All the cicadas sing.

x.

Jacmel, Haiti. Seashore. Salt-strewn air, billowing. Mouth of sand. Walk where freedmen walked. The ghosts of rebel slaves laughing and eating sugarcane. Their sweat waters these flowers still. Smell of poetry in the wind.

xi.

On a beach by the countryside, hibiscus blooms.

Eucharist

Corpus Christi
& the Saint Lucians are singing

        is the island real
            if you cannot see it ?

A mad frenzy of resorts
trees retreat from the shore

        everyone is a salesman , even the children
        we have erased them

tourist billboards a signifier
    for culture & Walcott weeps

        the thunderhead overflows
        with grief furious

    wet on the skin , echoing
    in the bones

& still

    the ocean is alive
    it eats & eats

        alien mountains devour the sky
          & the breath in Soufrière

is all sulphur it
   strangles the air

the music of Patwa
a harmony with Kreyòl

            hot stones underfoot swell with sun
            & burst —

   & you
are here beside me

        nodding at
      our siblings' quiet graves

          history has forgotten
        not us , not us

                I too fear erasure
            but   still

      disappear me
      into your mouth

          make me

                      holy

Portrait of Love as Revolution

> *"By your side, Camila"*
> —*Camila* (1984 Argentine film), dir. María Luisa Bemberg

When you are like this

    with me — legs crossed , lips

curled softly

    at the edges

like your hair , frizzy

    and wild

in the humid heat

    talking of power & revolution

politics & art

    poet-historians(Julia de Burgos ,

René Marques , Luis Rafael Sánchez —

    a litany of giants , daring

to record

    sinister silences

in empty rooms

    where dissidents voices once

echoed , disappeared

    to nothingness

& blood)

        the smothering invisible

American hand(they call him Adam Smith

)plucking the sun

from a wound of sky

        ,of tax havens & factories

cloying the bright air a chemical bruise

        US bombs dropped over Vieques

sickening rainbow fishes and ocean waters to ash

        & colonizer doctors bombing uterus and bone

so radioactive they glow

        blue in the dark(

what shines , incandescent

        cannot be hidden

from history)

        ,the mass graves of

independistas puertorriqueños

        boricua superheroes , romantics

who dreamed a colony one day

        freed

punched through with lead , ghostly

    corpses

mouthless & eyeless at the bottom

    of the sea , Rio Grande de Loíza

but no river

    can offer absolvement

for this —

    when you tell me

what it means

    for a Puerto Rican to be

away from her island , her womb

    a way a place a name

no one else remembers :

    at such moments I

cannot help

    but love you

Love Song for a Country

para mi Camila

Tall grass
swaying
in the golden sun
pastoral sustenance of cows
once the gods of men

Grey mist
crowding the air
in Humacao
flamboyán flowering
against the landscape
a mad flourish
of red

Mountain ridges
framing the sky
like the curves
of a beautiful green woman
nestled asleep on her side
and adrift
in a sea of crystal

I plunge
and swirl
in a blue
deep and profound
like the beauty
and pride
of a people
made strong by
the fisherman's hook &
the poet's blade

Night gathers
the moon opens

one pale eye
over Mayagüez
The coqui sings

We are dancing ,
swaying
My mouth is full
of ginger
and
your love

Your eyes
are a country
I will never leave

Ulysses Seeks Ithaca in the Antilles

        I.

Odysseus
never longed
for the cottage on the hill

        overlooking the ocean's surge —
        was never wistful
        for

almond & cherry trees
shaking in the breeze
or even

        screaming birds
        swelling the gulf
        the harbor in Saint-Marc

a mirror — silver
& pure
like its darting fish

        the prey of spears
        & the sky in it
        a miracle, luminous

& clear
like the face of God —
yes, Odysseus

        you
        who entered death
        & came back again

springing
from cracked earth
like bougainvillea

                    maddening
                    always
                    the coast

you, who chased
the moving
horizon

                    & fled
                    the anchor
                    of any island

bracing
the shore
& turning again & again

                    to the sea

you
never hungered
for home

                    never wept
                    to see again
                    that beach

where sun
turned you magic
made your skin

                    gleam
                    nor mourned
                    Elpenor

who will never see
again
that house he loved

                    stone licked white
                    by the waves
                    & yet —

II.

Yet I, too
have wandered
yearning

        for a memory
        I have only ever
        dreamed

seeking, under
the pattern in the cosmos
the stars overhead

        churning
        in the Atlantic's
        bath

no Laertes or Anticlea
but Haiti
my mother, my father

        & the stately palace
        in Ithaca
        my father's house

I will never see
though I have tried —
wrestling

        the laughing gods
        & unpiteous spirits
        a curse, a curse

on all my blood
the witch's evil eye
a furious hurricane's

        center
        the root of everything
        calamity

ever-present
fate's bulwark to return
& bitter tears

    feeding
    the garden
    the coconuts

like history
too heavy for
even the trees

    to bear
    thunderous
    like rain

in the crash
flood & famine
& the unforgiving earth

    opening its maw
    to swallow us & make
    a map of absence

the yearly
commonplace
apocalypse

    yet
    somehow, always
    the sea —

Ithaca, my Ithaca
these years I have pined
to see

    unlike that shadow my other
    you
    seeking

your salt-spray
& crunch of sand
underfoot

        the dilapidated buses
        your ships
        the corrugated roofs

a colonnade of palms
& even the city's
refuse

        a treasure
        some marker
        of place

for the weary
spurned from shore
to shore

        like the tide.

Homecoming

We return
heroic journeymen
one and by one

by boat and by plane: a migration
of sons and daughters
across azure seas

hearts unfearful
of the lunging waves or
coastal waters breaking with foam

We return
through thunder and lightning
the clamor of the lwas our gods

through memory and myth
our own tearful hesitancy
that treacherous storm

the trauma of history
Our vessels beach sand
and we disembark

harried and spent
redolent air dense
with heat

to touch hands
with our countrymen
& break cassava and bread

Tongues name & resurrect
dead men
from history's crypts

& past is present
among and within us
We relive them, we

slaves in the fields
catch the cracking whip
in the palm's sliced flesh

beat back battalions
& repossess the coast, we
shatter shackles and chains

under the clap of cannons
African gods our only shields
eucalyptus and castor oil our balms

our swords machetes & sugarcane
and palm trees our spears
bristling in the wind

against a blue dream of sky
We hear these roots
sing of blood

and are the fruits they bear
mango, its wet warm nectar
staining our mouths

audacious avocado, soft innards yellow
with love, yes love
Treeless mountain

We stamp your dry soil underfoot
occupying the crossroads
of our mothers and fathers

and weeping
for the toothless peasant farmer
the straw-hatted goat herder

the military juntas
shoeless children by the bay
scampering over rocks

and the unrealized ideal
of revolution
bright in the mind

like clear sun
filtered through crystal
O island our island embrace us

Meanwhile the sea
devours the shore
Time, time

impertinent irrefutable
time
Our phantom conjuring

collapses, dissolves
turns back to vapor
Back, back

we are swept back
through the years
returning

through communal remembrance
& generational imagining
We return, we return, weary

after peril & piteous journeying
having roamed the broad seas
to ourselves

& a reflection
in the ocean's mirror, our own hand
rippling it

Kreyòl

pou Hélène, pou Gran mwen

Hear
   the song of my people

      before it
         disappears

                      each utter
              a summoning

        to say
           remember me

                  remember Benin
          Africa's great

       walls
         or Dahomey

its fearsome
          amazons

     remember the speech
       of Anacaona

              Taíno flower
       of Yaguana —

ocean surf
an echoing

       our ancestors' curling
        tongues —

Fon & Wolof in each

  breath , each laugh

    each weep —
    they have survived

       in us , even
        under whip —

     bodies
      feeding the Atlantic —

slaves in the field
  cutting cane —

     the back's bunched
     muscles

       knots
        of Bantu —

     all of it
  frag

    ments
      & look

  look
    what we made of it

     look
     at our monuments —

not
   the fortress on the mountain

  revolution's
afterword

     nor the crumbling
   palace —

							gold glinting
								in light —

						not Vodou
				our gods —

							or even
					history's

		rupture
but

								music
					what music

in
	the eyes

					the hands
		what

power
in

							cheri
					kè mwen

											tout sa m fè
								pou ou —

														dear one
														my heart

														all that I do
														for you , for you

		— after horror
this language

                    of love —
            love our mythos

                            & fragments
                    only fragments

                                        of beauty

Veneration

My immigrant grandmother
in her winks & laughter
& stories of Vodou
teaching me everything
of Home ;

my French-reading father
adopting
strange American aphorisms
whose words
do not fit
the shape
of his mouth ;

my
(sweet,sweet like honey ,
like love)Creole-singing mother
filling the heavens with
her voice
in a language so beautiful
the stars sit to listen
& their tears fall
like meteors —

migrants
who have traversed
seas & boundaries & worlds

Haiti
       Puerto Rico
Cuba
       Nigeria
Vietnam
       Mexico
China

to come here

for the wisps of a dream
& I wonder
not if but how much
they've lost(

clear scattered sunlight ringing
        on the ocean
or the screaming rooster dancing at dawn
        neighbors' children playing in the street
car honks
        framed by dusty mountains
music with vibrant explosive rhythm &
        joy joy joy
the sugarcane cutters in the field
        coming in for coconut water
countrymen who speak their language
        &
whose tongues do not trip
        on the flavor of foods that taste
like memory
        mayi moulin ak sos pwa tembleque jollof bánh mì
& a people who know
        their country their identity their pride

)innumerable fragments
loosed to the wind , light & tenuous
like leaves
a handful of dust
but heavy
with the anchorage
of heritage
to connect us
across pages of history
and the trauma
of diaspora , which
is always
a violent dispersion —

all this

they've surrendered
without fear
without lamentation
and when I ask
wretched , pitiful , small
'why?'
that history
echoes
through their teeth
from within :

                                        for you

Flatbush and 7th Ave, 2021

Brooklyn again   streets shimmering with summer   Haitians and Dominicans and Trinidadians and Guyanans and Americans on Flatbush Ave eating Nashville hot finger-lickin' chicken   old immigrant men slamming down domino chips and crying triumph because nowadays every victory no matter how minor is valiant and deserving of vaunting   and who is blasting bachata and salsa at 1pm on a Thursday anyway   the natural music of our habitat swelling the air like birdsong   Yo son you stupid   You different kid   Get outta my face wit all that noise   You mad   Nah you big mad   Don't come round here no more shawty   What's good though like what's really good   son   Sun   hot on my neck burning my skin   cooking me blacker   color of the ocean at night   of the space between stars   blackness   that unfathomable birther of existence that origin of infinity   we are gods   and down the street isn't that that club where someone got stabbed one night   do you remember that night   that night we danced there furiously amid a mobbing sea of darkness   our feet pounding the wooden planks beneath us like drums and it was like we were summoning our ancestors   like we were our ancestors   our ancestors in chains aboard ships traversing the Atlantic   banging on floor boards scrabbling at walls wailing in terror   the sea a grave our only solace   torn from our mothers our fathers our lands and villages burned   our children raped   our hands our backs our bodies brutalized   our bloodlines obliterated   or so they tried   for here we are now   in this moment   each of us   descendants reconstructing our kinships making them new   conjuring that space in history's parentheses   now   now more than ever at the end of everything   in a world bereft of joy   a world of shattering earth and wildfire and plague and hysteria devouring the brain like fever   morgues brimming with our bodies   a cup runneth over   a world of floodwaters   water for Yemayá water for Mami Wata water for Maman Dlo water for Lasirenn   a prayer for all our deities   now   this now   we celebrate

Hymn to Haiti

    I.

Sing o muse

        — of what? This

is no hymn

        but the screaming

of a people flung

        to all corners of heaven

by dictatorship

        and imperialism

and a shattering earth

        a host of millions

out of chains   another Exodus

        across the waters

from

        those mountainous shores

to where?

    II.

Son of Haiti
child of an African god
broken over stone

splintered pieces
loosed to wind

— where are you?
in what land do you
find yourself?
to what land
do you crawl?

    III.

There is no more
home
Home
is a dream or memory
shored up of
fragments (

        dead poets
            and forgotten novels
        old music
            tasting of kompa
        and smelling of meringue
            and jazz ,
        mountains scattered
            with hyacinth
        & fortresses ,
            presidents
        no one remembers
            because France
        and America
            have buried their
        names —

silence
the past
& shape
power

) You search
for a dream
Dreamer :
where is the fantasy

Real?

    IV.

Real is
your breath
Your tongue's weight
the music of Kreyòl
Your grandmother's
cooking
Vodou stories
told over rum
ancient as Africa
in Haiti as in Puerto Rico
or Cuba
or Brasil
or Greece
for Ulysses also
slaughtered the ram
to counsel the dead

              Tell me : what is more real
              than ancestry?

    V.

Spirits
fly free
possess the flesh
drum music quickens
the heart
This is a song
that never dies
Home is a song

that never dies
Let it rise now inside you
let it crowd
your blood
lift your breast
burn your throat
like rum
and shake the stars —

We
are steel
tempered in fire
& wherever
we endure

is Home

Acknowledgements

My deepest thanks to the following journals, in which some of these poems first appeared, albeit sometimes in slightly different forms:

Apogee (Perigee Online): "Decolonization in the Context of Economic Dependence"

The Seventh Wave: "Diasporic Fever Dream"

Moko Magazine: "Re-Signification of Gold Grillz as War Helms," "In the light between being and becoming," and "Hymn to Haiti"

The Adirondack Review: "Veneration" and "Portrait of the Sea as"

Porridge Magazine: "After Basquiat" and "Dream Sequence with Fanon"

Tupelo Quarterly: "Banana Country: A Litany"

Sargasso: A Journal of Caribbean Literature, Language & Culture: "La Florida" and "Portrait of Love as Revolution"

Grateful to have written this narrative of (im)migration. Thank you to the poets, novelists, and playwrights who have most poignantly shaped me: Derek Walcott, René Depestre, Frankétienne, Marie Vieux-Chauvet, Jacques Roumain, Jacques Stéphen Alexis, Kei Miller, Audre Lorde, Ezra Pound, HD, ee cummings, Gabriel García Márquez, Roberto Bolaño, and so, so many more. More importantly, thank you to my Haitian and African ancestors, for surviving all this way. Thank you to my mother and grandmother, Marie-Ange Rancy née Milord and Hélène Milord née Séide; and thank you my sister, Jemille Tangela Rancy; and to my father, Jean-Claude Rancy; to my dear cousins, Marlev Adonis, Jeffrey Casimir, Baverly Fleuranville, Macabnel Adonis, Bobby Milord, Helena Desir, Prisca Felix, Priscilla Felix, Shaquina Pagenel—to my family: a lineage, a bloodline. Thank you, Camila Pérez Santiago, my Camila, my first and greatest reader, the speaker of a nation, the greatest of artists. An immortalization of all your names, which only literature can do.

Born to Haitian immigrants in South Florida, **SK RANCY** is a writer of diaspora. He received his BA in English & Comparative Literature and Biology from Columbia University. His poetry has been longlisted for Button Poetry's Chapbook Contest and a finalist for Tupelo Quarterly's Poetry Prize. He has been published or is forthcoming in *Columbia New Poetry, Intima: A Journal of Narrative Medicine, Ars Medica, Apogee, The Seventh Wave, Moko Magazine, The Adirondack Review, Porridge Magazine,* and *Sargasso: A Journal of Caribbean Literature, Language & Culture*. His unpublished novel BEYOND THE BATHS OF STARS was selected as a semi-finalist for Black Lawrence Press's The Big Moose Prize and a finalist for the University of New Orleans' Publishing Laboratory Contest. His poetry and other writings largely focus on black identity, Caribbean diaspora, and immigration, as well as ontology, medicine, and human morality as viewed through the critical lens of history. In his spare time, he is a surgical resident. He lives in New York.

www.ingramcontent.com/pod-product-compliance
Lightning Source LLC
Chambersburg PA
CBHW031126160426
43192CB00008B/1129